UNWINDING ROAD

some poems

a *story*

CHRISTINE BIENKO

Unwinding Road
Copyright © 2021 by Christine Bienko

Illustrations by Salvatore Oggiano
Layout Design by Anielika Sykes

All rights reserved. No part of this publication may be reproduced, distributed, or transmitted in any form or by any means, including photocopying, recording, or other electronic or mechanical methods, without the prior written permission of the author, except in the case of brief quotations embodied in critical reviews and certain other non-commercial uses permitted by copyright law.

Tellwell Talent
www.tellwell.ca

ISBN
978-0-2288-5698-6 (Paperback)
978-0-2288-6183-6 (eBook)

To my late parents
John and Marianne
know that I paid attention

to my late brother Richard
thank you for paving the way

to my daughter Anielika
you are now and ever
my sunshine

your lives are my inspiration.

CONTENTS

SOME-
WHERE

TO

START

the road goes ever on and on
down from the door where it began

- J.RR. Tolkien

why

the hardest part is
to start somewhere then find your
way and reach the end

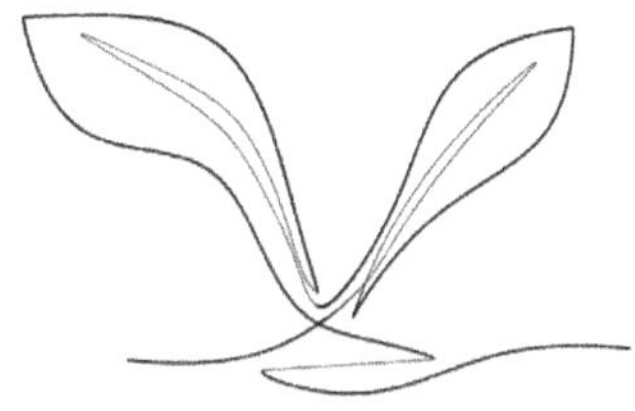

why not

if i knew myself
life would be so much simpler
the search continues

what if

it may be worthwhile
to keep fighting the good fight
someone has to win

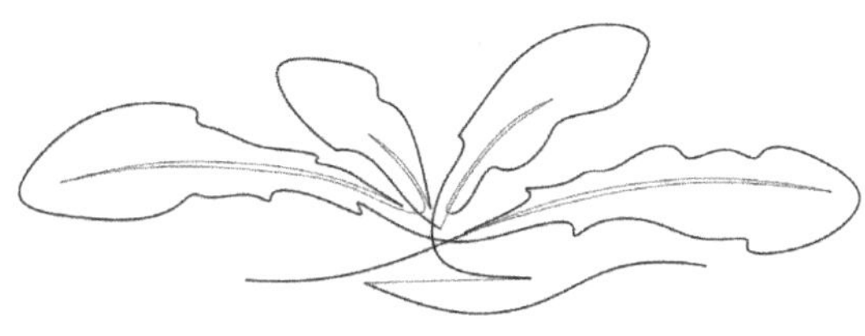

when

seek until you find
keep searching until the end
is clearly in sight

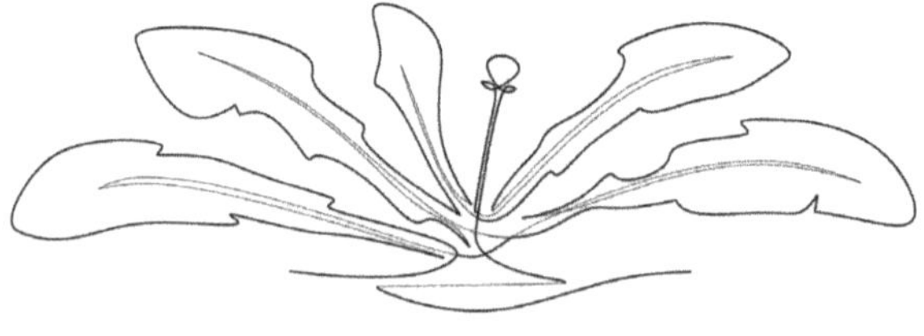

where

the journey begins
with a dream long to become
someone different

Destination

Starting begins
with an impulse
a need to reach
beyond my skin

to see the sky
above my head
to feel the ground
beneath my feet

to strive with
my head and
seek with my heart

trusting I am
heading somewhere
worth being.

A Glimpse

Obscuring the obvious
mist hovers like a film
before my eyes
tenuous in its hold
on what otherwise
might be clear

guessing at best
what lies ahead
I doubt each step

suspending trust
with each step
eyes closed
I see the obvious.

Snapshot

Time caught
frozen
snapped in place

a smile
a touch
a tear

unnoticed then
remembered now

it was something
it was nothing

ageless timeless
treasures.

Bruised Innocence

At first love feels
soft and warm
safe in the promise
of care and hope
and growing old

at first anger feels
hard and cold
and unforgiving.

It is this way at first
bruising a view
of the world
that starts small.

In a world no longer small
love matter most.

Patchwork

Unchecked words
linger restless
and willful
memory full
and overfull
of words that
undermine and
overwhelm
unthinking words
said once
unsettling

fractured upended
words dance
in my brain
late at night.

Sleepless I weigh
them all and edit
what I need to keep
storing the rest
for another day.

Imprint

I turn the pages
one by one
filled with stories
held in place
by some look
that begs to be
understood

secrets and sorrows
hidden behind
a smile
not quite certain
caught just so

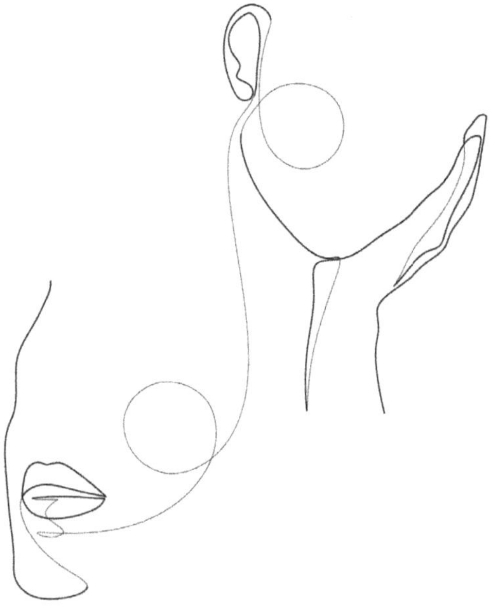

I pause with care
longing to see
bits of who I was and
who I may become.

Limbo Life

I find you in
your room alone
lost in thought

I enter and
take my place
nearby waiting
to hear once more
the telling
of another life.

You left for love
and promises

you left to write
a new story
a different story
your own story.

It was not what
you expected.

Reflection

Light breaks
tears fall
the day begins
I shudder

slow and dull
my eyes adjust
to nothing

only this

her eyes in
mine her
heart undone
my sad
and lonely
mother.

Just Enough

Brisk steps taken
with purpose
each more driven
than the next
whatever the task
whatever the goal
his steps were brisk

eyes fixed forward
I followed close
behind afraid
to fall behind
small feet running
to keep up.

There were times
when he let me
fall in step
to look up
and see the
faintest smile
letting me catch
the hint of love
he guarded like
a treasure.

In time
it was enough.

Confession

Grappling with
competing images
troubling at best

urgency forces
me to speak
and clear my heart.

It is not easy.

Unlikely Twins

You did not ask
for me but
I came anyway
wanted as kids
are wanted
no more no less

we grew as one
close in ways
that could not be
explained.

You were the first
mapping the way
for me as I followed
in your shadow
keeping my place
in the distance.

Death pulled you
into a shadow
I could not
follow even from
a distance.

If I could I would
tell you that
I did not mind
being in your
shadow

but then
maybe you knew
that all along.

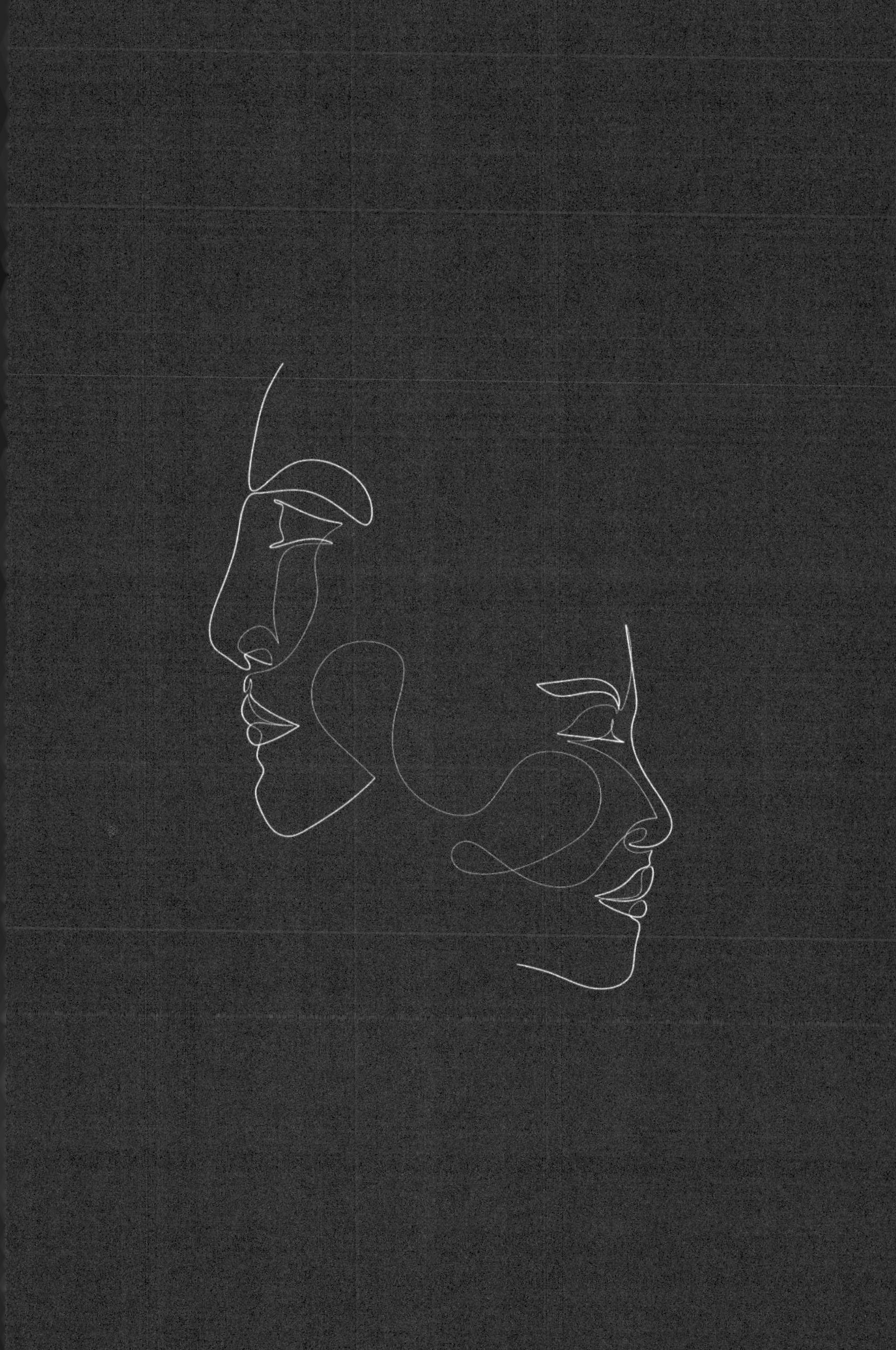

Still life

Loud noise cuts
into my calm
upsetting unravelling
late night noise
outside noise
lead to wakeful
nights and hard
memories that
do not fade
the need to hide
does not fade.

At times the noise
of life around me
is simply too much
so I hide to feel the
comfort of a secret
place where I can
sit alone restored
by the stillness.

Saving Grace

Time and again
words save me
well-scripted words
with some twist
of a dare some
lure of desire
words play me
like an idle
drum begging
to be struck
with passion
and promise

some days
a sad tale
some days
a fairy tale
always a tale
that lifts me
up beyond
the ordinary.

Forecast

At the start
nothing is clear
the road ahead
wide open
destiny a dream
within reach

at the start
one chapter folds
into the next
a story in the
making.

The end lies
hidden at the
start waiting.

At Peace

Hands rest gently
in my lap
breath soft
silent movement
in sync with
each heartbeat
each fluttered
eyelid.

The waiting is
painless.

Early Evening

Young women
do not walk alone
but I did
leaving home for awhile
I walked

at times to clear my head
at times to simply
feel a sense of going
somewhere on my own
to be alone.

Most often to a nearby
park where an endless
stretch of open sky
and tall trees waited
where a duck pond
waited.

I sat content to be
a young woman alone.

MAYBE

THE

MIDDLE

"my eyes already touch the sunny hill
going far beyond the road i have begun,
so we are grasped by what we cannot grasp;
it has an inner light…and changes us…"

- Rainer Maria Rilke

if then

uncertain at times
unwavering steps persist
as the road unwinds

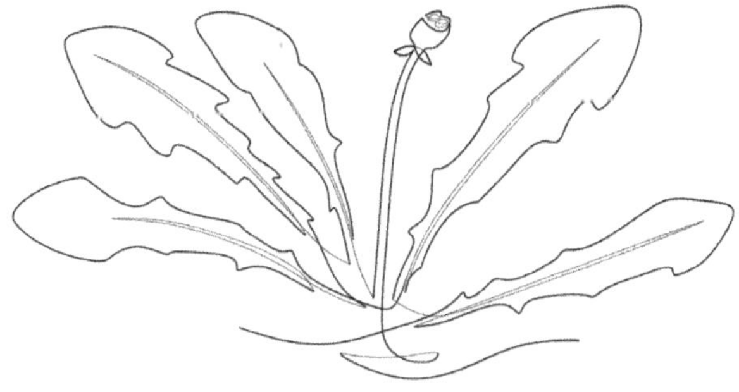

then what

shattered in pieces
faith falters light dims too soon
fallen and broken

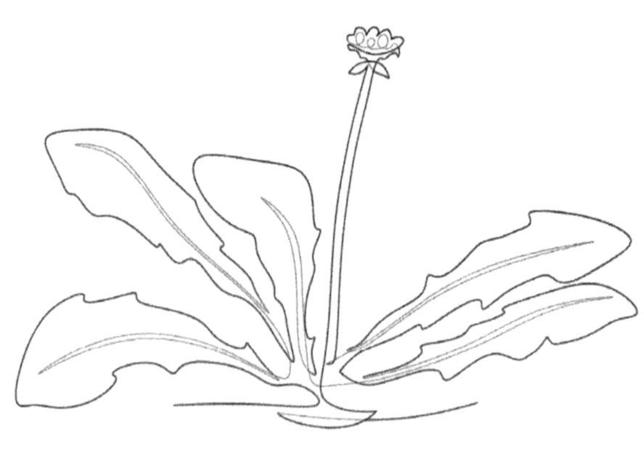

then where

weary thoughts spinning
tears wear me down numb and frail
lost until sleep comes

then how

fragments of light slow
and steady nudge me forward
forcing me to hope

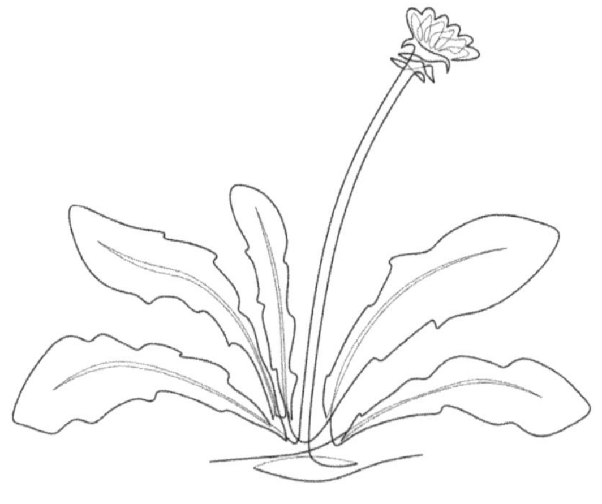

maybe then

until you can stand
let me hold you in my arms
loving you fiercely

Shifting Gears

My steps are
rarely even
love and loss
make it hard
to stay upright
to stay clear and
navigate the
proverbial fork
in the road

footing falters
steps are traced
and retraced
the way forward
confused with the
way back blurring
the plan shifting
steps taken.

Stay the Course

Endless searching
beginning to end
from growing up
to growing old
from birth to death

passion played
and passion cooled
the first dance
feeling much like
the last but slower
and softer

lost and found
but not quite lost
misplaced now
and again.

Finally found
in the beginning.

Phantom Love

Time stumbled
upon itself
the day you died
numb with grief
I held our child
shallow breath
straining
to be still
to be calm

voice fragments
sounding like
a pulse in my ear
your voice saying
only this

Live.

That Day

It was a day to last
all days with love
declared before others
promises made
to have and to hold
promises made
believing love would
last forever.

On that day
I was someone
I would not know now
expecting less
accepting less.

I see you still
as you were
on that day
beaming with joy
until death
did us part.

Christine Bienko

Endurance

Disquiet churns
within testing
my will
to stay standing

by design
or misdirection
footing is lost

I will not break
I will not fall.

The will to stay
standing is
everything.

Easy Prey

You see me
in the distance
and catch my eye
your smile inviting
urging me to stop
and listen

you tell me
what I want to hear
what I need to hear
about myself
noticing me simply
for passing by.

I sit and listen
caring less about the
words you say
caring more about
your tone of voice
pretending to care
for a woman
simply passing by.

You show me what
you sell saying
I will feel pretty
I will feel noticed

your fingers
pat my cheek
tapping gently
tapping softly

you stand back
and stare waiting
for me to speak.

Your touch still
warm upon my skin
I smile and
walk away.

Endless Dream

Suspended between
life and not-life
reaching back
to remember
to pull back
someone loved
and lost like
a precious pebble

I resist the waking
resist the coming
back into unsorted
stories and then
let go.

Self-Edit

In stillness
equal parts of joy
and pain prevail

breathe in
breathe out

descending within
cuts into what
holds me back
slowly I arise

a moment of grace
ascends finding
me waiting.

Choose Me

Your small voice calls
out softly as I leave
sadness muted
choose me

sadness fills me
torn as always
by the leaving

we make it through
the day and all the days
neither one the worse
for wear.

I hear it still
your small voice calling
soft and sad and muted
choose me.

And I do.

Unmasked

It took some time to show
the less than perfect
part of me
the part that cried
lonely and afraid
when you were young

the part that stood by
as you pulled back
silenced by a bad dream
or a broken heart

the part that cracked
when you grew up
and moved away
pretending to be strong
and happy.

Older now I smile to hear
you did not fail to see
the less than perfect part.

You loved me all the same.

Buried Secret

Dull ache piercing
deep in my gut
memory cloaked
in darkness

silence stills
the pain of what
remains unsaid
buried in folds
of regret and missed
opportunities.

Tightrope

Another night awaits
brain burning
twitching on the
brink of rest
words spoken
and unspoken
upon waking
dangle like puzzle
pieces abandoned
and unsolved
in the darkness
blurred images spin
faces known and
unknown broken
conversations
unended waiting.

At last dawn beckons.
Another day begins.

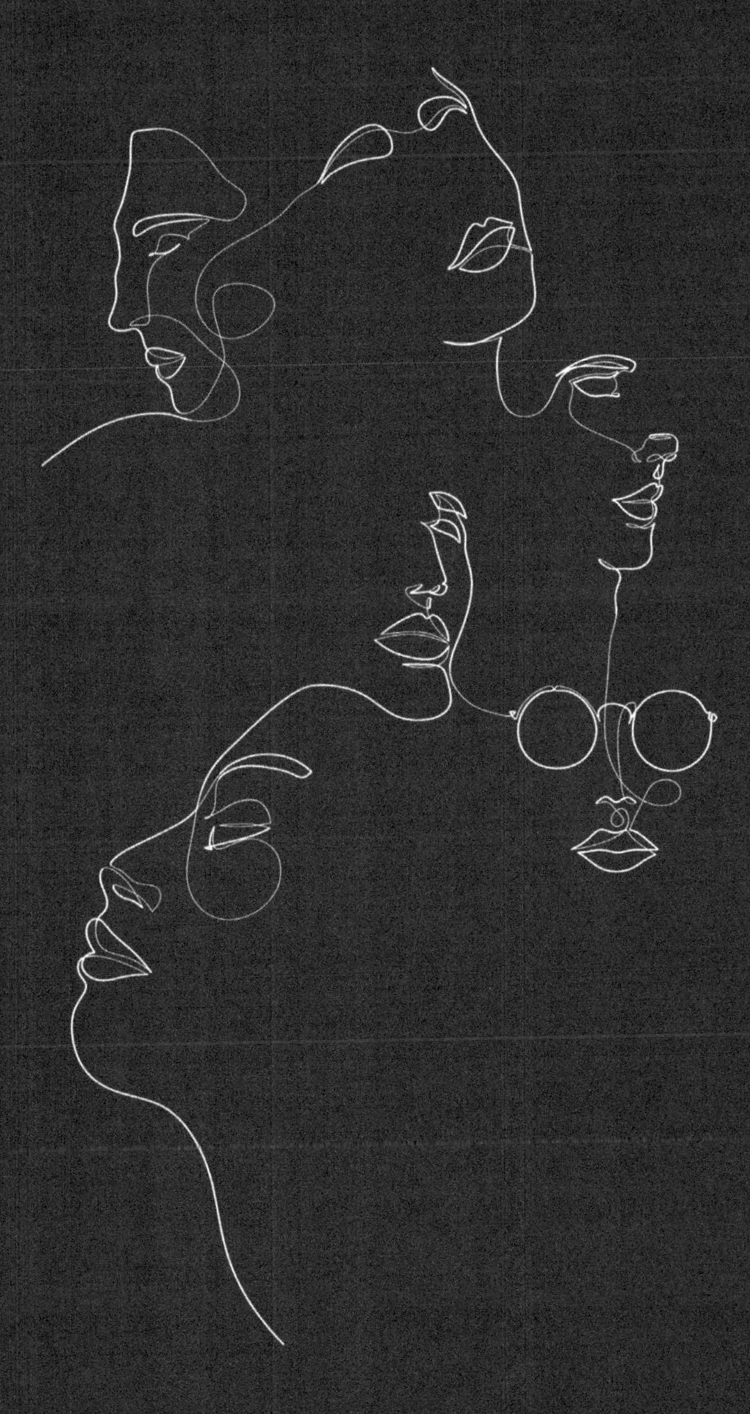

Unexpected

It happens
so quickly
balance lost

I fall

unnerved angry
fists punch the air
a scream caught
in my gut

dazed unsure of
what next

I lie still

afraid to move
unhinged unnerved

I lie still
helpless confused
abandoned to myself.

Rage spreads
to aching limbs
willing me to crawl
slowly painfully
reaching blindly
for something
to pull me up.

Dumb thoughts surface

Where is my phone?
Who do I call?
What do I say?

Shame is my undoing
I will say nothing
tell no one.

It is just a fall.

Fallen Limbs

It stood outside my window
for years admired
for its simple beauty
tall green branches
spread majestically
inviting simple wonder
as I sat at the corner
kitchen window sipping
an early morning coffee
or evening tea
neighbours stopping by
to look and smile.

Some miscue
cut my tree in a day
years of watching
me watching gone.

Levelled dirt remains
a grave for what stood once
outside my kitchen window.

Empty House

The house that
knew me well
stands still and silent
as I stare

we are no more
the kids and mom
and dad all gone

family photos
boxed linen
folded worn and
treasured

walls and windows
stripped bare
ghost like and
unfamiliar.

Rooms now empty
echo with sounds
of babies crying
family meals
and too many
disagreements.

It all replays
as if alive
relived one last time.

I see it all
and save it all
then leave it all behind.

Encrypted

Virtual life
traps me
images forever
drawing me
into blind alleys
teasing me with
scraps of knowing
the world as it is
and may be

no one truth prevails
lost in links
spilling into other
links splintered
fog-like threads
that never end.

Lovely woods
on a snowy night
calm and sacred
save me.

Just so

I fold into myself
one year at a time
one day at a time
each hour
each moment
seeing something different
feeling something different

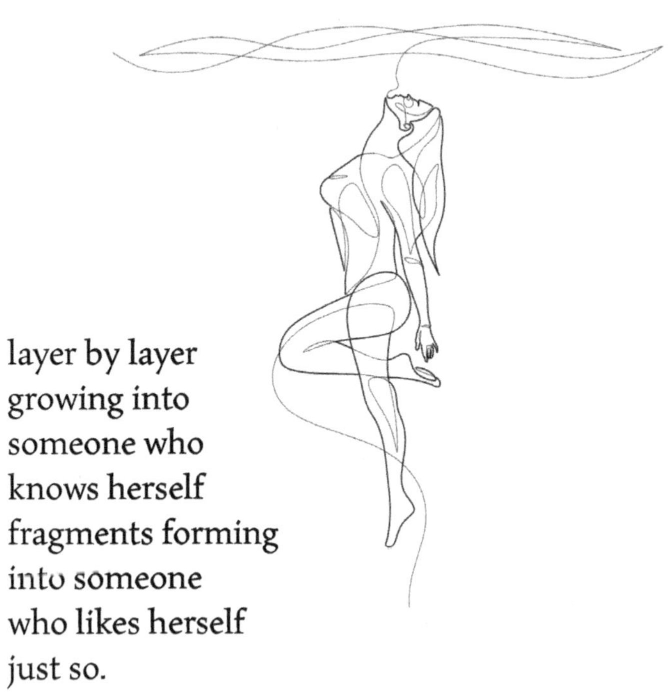

layer by layer
growing into
someone who
knows herself
fragments forming
into someone
who likes herself
just so.

NOT

THE

END

"do not go gently into that good night,
rage, rage against the dying of the light."

- Dylan Thomas

what is

unbroken and fierce
destined from the beginning
whatever the end

what then

i will stay the course
in pain in tears at times lost
i dare to matter

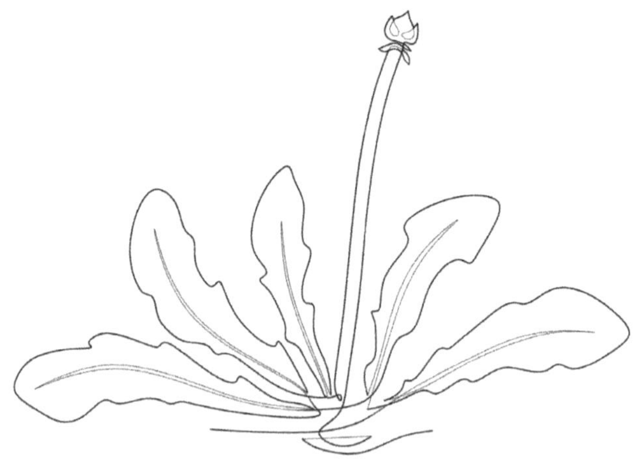

what more

the story we live
unfolds layer by layer by layer
the ending matters

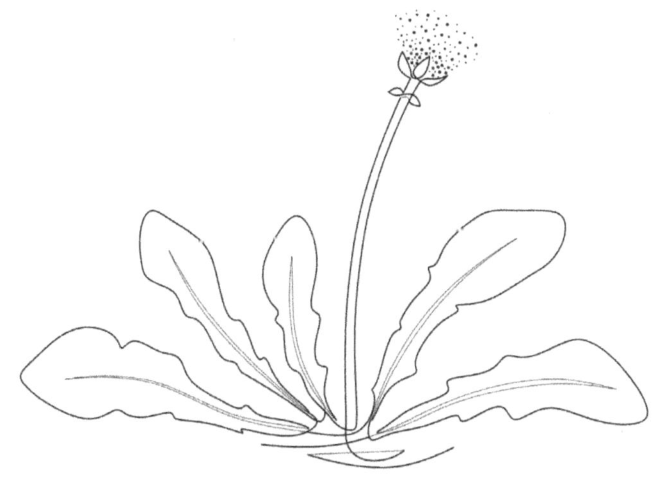

what becomes

let go to let be
to become is to let go
at one and at peace

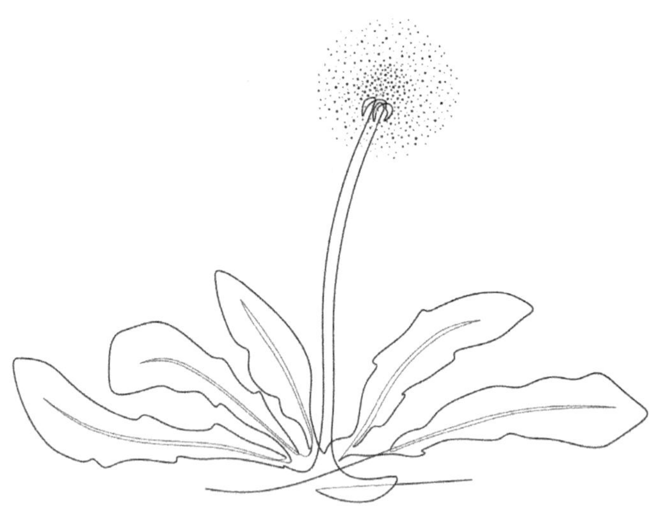

what next

delicate balance
sightless movement unfolding
one step at a time

All In

It drifts within reach
but not quite
an old boat
cradled in still
waters waiting

I am not ready
travelling this
great distance
I am afraid
to step forward
afraid to get in.

Reaching for
the hand extended
I make my way
eyes closed
mind open.

Then I take
my place.

Readiness

Calm abiding stirs
the noise within
stilling the sound
gentle and patient

resisting I struggle
to say yes
to let go
of the clouds
in my head

calm abiding waits
until I am ready
to say yes
enter.

Bravado

One day I walk
slowly each step
taken with care
uncertain and
unnoticed

other days I walk
briskly and determined
with each step taken
trusting my gut
knows I am heading
somewhere worth
being

then there are
days when I
simply fake it
and just keep
walking.

Rooftops

A blanket of rooftops
stretch before me
each one different
blending one into the other
a tapestry of lives
safely tucked within
weather-worn walls
stained by the seasons
unaffected and secure
in the place
they were planted.

Something within
me stirs comforted
by the constancy
of the rooftops
shielding the lives
lived within.

Detour

Perched and still
a seagull waits
calm and sure
until I notice
one eye fixed on me
as I sit and watch
the bits of bread
I tossed before
now gone

head tilted
its one eye stares
as if to ask

Is there more?

I smile back sadly
and shake my head.

Unfazed the small
white head turns
away abruptly

feathers flash in flight
my friend takes off
never looking back.

Framed

We are a group
of travellers
cameras ready
for the perfect
pose the perfect
smile mindful
of shadows that
block the perfect
place to stand

alone I save
my smile for what
I see eyes cast
freely feet
planted safely
in the shadows.

Embers

Unnoticed until
I step inside
thoughts fall back
to another time
a place like this
where strangers
come to pray

their silent words
muttered in hope
and secret longing
to be lifted up
beyond a promise
and a prayer.

Once blind
trust moved me.

Older now
I simply sit
and listen.

Hard Stones

My pilgrim feet
walk the cobbled
streets of sacred
places taking in
the many signs
of what it looks
like to believe
in something
greater than me
something unseen.

I see it all
stone walls
built with care
stained glass
windows lit
by candles
from within.

In the distance
a young woman
kneels on hard stones
eyes cast down
paper cup in hand
patiently waiting
in the rain as
pilgrims pass
her by.

Fine Balance

Shards of rock
crunch beneath
my feet cutting
into the soles
of my shoes.

How did I come
to stumble
upon this path?

Lost I carry on
there is no other
way forward.

Under the Stars

Secrets spin beneath
the stars embedded
in a darkened sky

standing alone
I gaze upward
bits of brilliant light
gazing back

fate and fortune
cast their light in turn
bedazzling as I stare
yearning to know
how life unfolds
and why.

It is this way with secrets.

I am content to simply
look up and wonder.

Ever After

Good stories
never die
heroes fight
the good fight
love prevails
lives change
for better or worse
they change.

My story is not
great but good
enough to tell
no heroes lose
or save the day
love did not
prevail but lasted
long enough
I have fought
the good fight.

It is a story
worth telling.

Corner Table

Conversations flow
as I step unnoticed
into the small
dimly lit café
expecting no one
expected by no one

I find my place
in the corner
a table set for one
a table with a view.

Glancing up I see
the passersby
lost in idle
cell phone chatter.

I watch them
secretly without
regret sipping
wine alone at
my corner table.

An Evening Out

Older women
do not walk alone
but I do
far from home
I step out and walk
the evening air
a calm companion

not knowing the way
draws me forward eager
to see something different
to be somewhere different.

Street lights turn into
river lights making
me stop and look
at the wonder
of a night sky
far from home content
to be an older woman
walking alone.

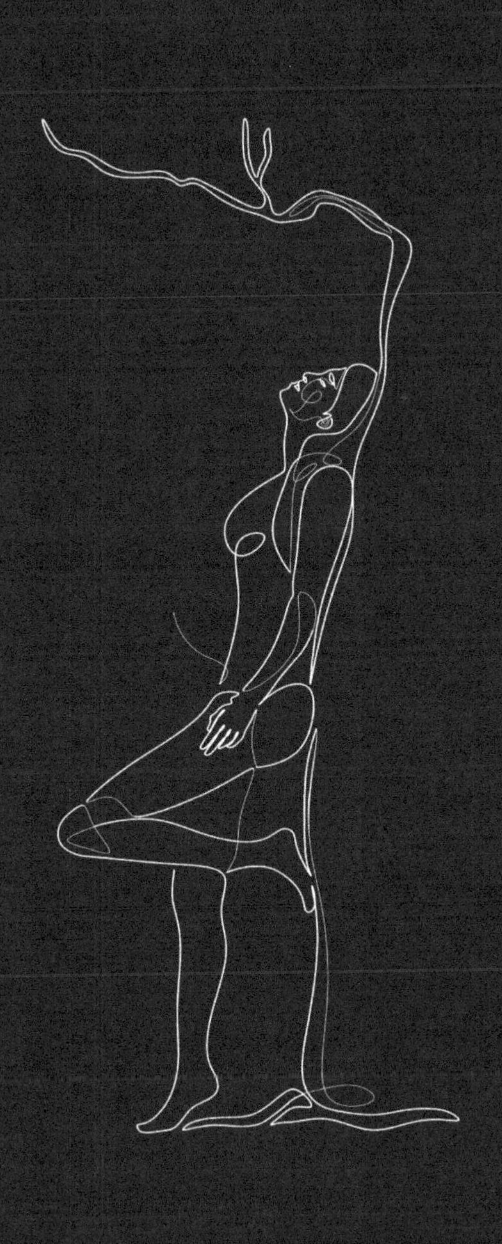

Captive (Fado)

Eyes closed
body swaying
he plays as if for me
pulsing life into
songs that speak
of destiny and despair
songs of broken
dreams and love

he does not see me
yet somehow
knows I am swept
up in the piercing
notes of longing
raw and intimate
his fingers pluck fiercely
and I sway eyes closed
struck by the glimpse
of pain in my soul.

Last Life

I lived before
at least once
another time
another place
as someone else

it was not
a better life nor
a lesser life

it was simply
another life
as someone else.

I am forever
on my way
to becoming
different.

Begin Again

Each tale unfolds
in its own time
in its own way

one laden with
sadness twisted
by turns of fate
and calamity

one candid and
ripe for telling
born whole
from beginning
to end.

My tale seems
to linger incomplete
begging to begin
again.

Christine Bienko has been an educator for the better part of her professional life. She has written numerous poems and short articles. Christine lives in Mississauga, Ontario. This is her first book.